BIOFUELS

by Patricia Newman

ENERGY LAB:
BIOFUELS

CHERRY LAKE PUBLISHING • ANN ARBOR, MICHIGAN

CHERRY LAKE Publishing

Published in the United States of America
by Cherry Lake Publishing
Ann Arbor, Michigan
www.cherrylakepublishing.com

Printed in the United States of America
Corporate Graphics Inc.
January 2013
CLFA10

Consultants: D. Leith Nye, Education and Outreach Specialist, Great Lakes Bioenergy Research Center; Marla Conn, reading/literacy specialist and educational consultant

Editorial direction: Lauren Coss   Book design and illustration: Emily Love

Photo credits: Lars Timm/Fotolia, cover, 1; Shutterstock Images, Design Element (all); Kent Sorensen/Shutterstock Images, 5; Red Line Editorial, 7; Library of Congress, 9; Sharon Morris/Shutterstock Images, 11; LiteChoices/Shutterstock Images, 13; Fotolia, 15; Jon Meier/iStockphoto, 18; Jim Parkin/Shutterstock Images, 20; Nagel Photography/Shutterstock Images, 22; Martin Pateman/Shutterstock Images, 25; Renee Bucci/Bigstock, 27

Library of Congress Cataloging-in-Publication Data
Newman, Patricia, 1958-
  Biofuels / Patricia Newman.
    pages cm. — (Energy lab)
  Audience: 8-9
  Audience: Grade 4 to 6
  Includes bibliographical references and index.
  ISBN 978-1-61080-893-4 (hardback : alk. paper) — ISBN 978-1-61080-918-4 (paperback : alk. paper) — ISBN 978-1-61080-943-6 (ebook) — ISBN 978-1-61080-968-9 (hosted ebook)
1. Biomass energy—Juvenile literature. I. Title.

TP339.N495 2013
333.95'39—dc23

2012030463

Cherry Lake Publishing would like to acknowledge the work of The Partnership for 21st Century Skills. Please visit www.21stCenturySkills.org for more information.

TABLE OF CONTENTS

You are being given a mission. The facts in What You Know will help you accomplish it. Remember the clues from What You Know while you are reading the story. The clues and the story will help you answer the questions at the end of the book. Have fun on this adventure!

Scientists are constantly looking for ways to improve our sources of energy. They want to discover how to produce energy that is more efficient, less expensive, and better for the environment than our current energy sources. Your mission is to learn more about biofuels. What are they? How do we use them today? How might we use them in the future? Read the facts in What You Know and start learning about the exciting world of biofuels!

WHAT YOU KNOW

★ Alternative energy research tries to balance our energy needs with the need to protect our environment.

★ Fossil fuels such as gasoline and diesel are made of **organic** material. This material is buried underground for millions of years. Fossil fuels are nonrenewable. We are using them up more quickly than they are created.

★ Modern biofuels take much less time to make than fossil fuels.

Corn is a biomass that is already an important part of meeting our energy needs.

★ Biofuels are made from biomass. Organic material or living things are biomass.

★ Biofuels are liquid fuels used for transportation. Biofuels are made from renewable organic material.

Pete Linsley is researching biofuels as part of an article he is writing for his school's newspaper. He is meeting with energy experts and farmers to learn more about how biofuels might fit into our energy future. Carry out your mission by reading his journal.

The first place I go is my uncle Dan's house. He is a middle school science teacher. I think he might know a thing or two about biomass. He's in the garage working under his car. The car is raised, and I can see his feet and blue jeans sticking out from underneath.

"Uncle Dan, can you tell me a little about biomass?" I ask.

"Take a look in that big garbage can," he responds, still under the car. I walk over to the big plastic garbage can. It is full of yard waste. I see grass clippings, leaves, wood chips—even an apple core. (I guess someone got hungry while they were working!)

Uncle Dan slides out from under the car. "Everything in that garbage can is biomass," he explains. "Biomass is organic material made from plants and animals. All that yard waste is organic material." He tells me that organic material stores and provides energy in an endless cycle. Plants and animals take in oxygen and give off carbon dioxide. Plants absorb the carbon dioxide and turn it into energy during **photosynthesis**. During photosynthesis, plants use the sun's energy and carbon dioxide to make food for themselves. When plants do this, they give off oxygen.

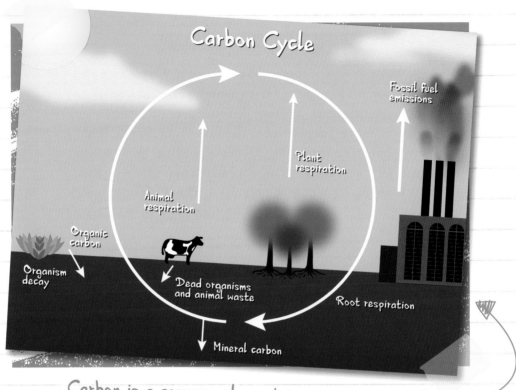

Carbon Cycle

Fossil fuel emissions

Plant respiration

Animal respiration

Organic carbon

Organism decay

Dead organisms and animal waste

Root respiration

Mineral carbon

Carbon is a common element in organic materials.
Too much carbon can lead to climate change.

Animals breathe the oxygen and eat the plants. The animals breathe out carbon dioxide. The cycle starts all over again. Biomass stores some of this energy, which can be used as food for humans and animals. Biomass can also be used to meet human energy needs.

"Every day you throw away biomass that could be used to create energy," Uncle Dan says. "Biomass has the ability to become liquid fuel. We can use that wasted energy to help cut back on our need for nonrenewable energy sources, such as oil or petroleum."

BURNING BIOMASS

Do you have a fireplace in your house? Wood is a common form of biomass. When wood burns in your fireplace, it releases energy in the form of heat. Wood emits more carbon into the air than fossil fuels such as gasoline. However, unlike gasoline the carbon released by burning wood is already part of the carbon cycle, so no new carbon is released. Still, wood smoke contains harmful pollutants that can be bad for the environment.

Uncle Dan points to his car. "This car runs on gasoline like most modern cars," he says. "But biofuels, or fuels made from biomass, have been around for a long time. When Henry Ford sold his first Model T car in 1908, he planned to fuel it with ethanol, a type of alcohol made from corn or other energy-producing crops. Early diesel engines ran on peanut oil, a kind of biomass, rather than gasoline. In fact, gasoline was a waste substance left over from the production of kerosene, a type of oil used in lanterns before electricity was common. Ford's Model T changed everything. Gasoline became the fuel of choice because it was cheap. It released a burst of energy when it burned."

Fossil fuels such as petroleum that are used to make gasoline are very old biomass. They are made from plants

Ford's Model T car was originally designed to run on ethanol.

and animals buried underground. Then they are cooked by the earth's heat and pressure over millions of years. Because fossil fuels take so long to make, we use them up more quickly than they can be created. "Petroleum is becoming more expensive as it becomes less plentiful," Uncle Dan says. "Besides, digging fossil fuels from the ground and burning them sends extra carbon elements into the environment in the form of carbon dioxide. Extra carbon can disturb the balance of earth's delicate carbon cycle. This can lead to climate change."

"Today's biofuels speed up the time it takes to produce fuel," my uncle says. "Instead of waiting millions of years, modern biofuel can be made in months."

"If biofuels are so great, why haven't they replaced gasoline?" I ask.

"Gasoline contains more energy per gallon than biofuel. It's a good deal more efficient in most modern cars."

"Meaning we get more miles per gallon when we drive, right?" I say.

"Right," Uncle Dan says. "Although changes in engine technology could make biofuels almost as efficient as gasoline. But we still have to learn how to manufacture enough biofuels for the whole world."

Uncle Dan invites me in for some cookies, but I have to get going. I still have questions about biofuels. He said that early cars were designed to run on ethanol. But where does ethanol come from? ★

I remember the apple core in Uncle Dan's garbage can. Food is biomass too. I decide to visit my mom's college roommate in Iowa to check out a cornfield. I ride past miles and miles of cornfields occasionally dotted by farmhouses. Before I know it, I'm standing with farmer Mary Chen in the middle of her cornfield. The stalks are higher than our heads, and they have fat ears with golden corn silk. They look tasty, but Mary sells her corn for fuel instead of food.

"Corn has fed the world for centuries," she says. "Now it's fueling the world with ethanol. We use the same

Corn is used for food and to create fuel.

planting and harvesting techniques whether our corn becomes food or ethanol. First we plant the corn seeds. Next we fertilize and water them. Then we harvest them."

Mary explains that ethanol is the only biofuel currently available on a large scale. Right now, ethanol makes up approximately 10 percent of the U.S. fuel supply. Basically, ethanol is the same kind of alcohol as in the beer or liquor adults drink. This alcohol can be mixed with gasoline. Then it helps reduce **greenhouse gases** that contribute to global warming.

I look at the ears of corn all around me. "Do you make the ethanol here on the farm?"

SUGARCANE

Instead of using corn to make the ethanol, Brazilians use one of their most common crops—sugarcane. Sugarcane contains sucrose sugar in its stalk. Sucrose is the type of sugar you might find on your table. Sugar is one of the favorite foods of certain ethanol-producing microbes. Sugarcane might be an even better way to create ethanol than corn. Corn must be replanted every year. But sugarcane only needs to be replanted every six years. Today, approximately 90 percent of Brazilian vehicles run on a mixture of gasoline and ethanol.

Sugarcane is an important crop in many parts of the world. Some countries create ethanol with it.

Mary shakes her head. "We harvest the corn and grind up the kernels. Then we ship the corn to a factory. Corn is usually more than 70 percent starch, a type of **carbohydrate**. The factory converts the starch to sugars using **enzymes**. These **proteins** help speed up a chemical reaction. Once the corn starch has been broken down, tiny organisms called microbes eat the sugars," she says. "These microbes produce ethanol as they munch away."

"Why can't we just fill our gas tanks with ethanol?"
I ask.

"Like gasoline, ethanol is not a perfect fuel," Mary says. "First of all, the energy content is low. You need about one and one half gallons (5.7 L) of ethanol to equal the energy power of one gallon (3.8 L) of gasoline. Second, it mixes with water."

I already know that petroleum is an oil-based product. I remember from science class that oil and water do not mix. But I don't understand why ethanol mixing with water is bad.

"First, water doesn't burn," Mary says. "Additionally, water messes up the way engines work. It weakens the energy content of the fuel."

Mary tells me that some people worry about what will happen to food production if more and more farmers use their fields to plant crops for ethanol rather than for food. If the demand for corn for both food and fuel goes up, corn prices will also go up. This can affect other food prices. Cattle often eat corn. If farmers have to pay more for the corn to feed their cattle, the price of beef might also go up.

Mary adds, "But ethanol has still saved your parents money. Ethanol prices are lower than gasoline. And ethanol-gasoline blends are very common now. Ethanol-gasoline

If more corn is used to make ethanol, food prices could rise.

makers keep finding more efficient ways to create the blends. Not all ethanol is made from corn grain," she adds. "Ethanol can also be made from corn leaves and stalks. Ethanol made from plants such as switchgrass or sugarcane could be the ethanol of the future!" ★

Today I am visiting switchgrass farmer Tom Felix at his field in Oklahoma. As I get close, I notice long grass bordering both sides of the road. It is much taller than I am.

Tom greets me with a warm smile. "Hi, Pete. Welcome to our switchgrass field. All of the grass on our farm is used to make biofuel. Switchgrass is great because it grows on just about any type of land. It doesn't need prime farmland with excellent soil the way corn does. Switchgrass grows back after it's harvested too. We don't need to replant it every year."

The grass grows in rows like corn, but the rows are much closer together.

"Switchgrass produces advanced biofuel," Tom says. "It is full of **cellulose**, a type of carbohydrate." I remember Mary's field, where I learned enzymes can convert carbohydrates into sugars. When microbes eat the sugars, they create ethanol. Tom continues, "The high cellulose content of the grass produces more fuel per acre than corn. One acre's worth of corn grain can produce approximately 400 gallons (1,500 L) of fuel, but an acre of switchgrass can produce approximately 1,000 gallons (3,800 L) of fuel."

THE BUILDING BLOCKS OF BIOFUELS

Carbon is the key ingredient in the creation of biofuels. Ethanol is a compound, or a substance made of two or more elements. Ethanol contains approximately 70 percent of the energy in a gallon of gasoline. Butanol is a compound made from switchgrass or other biomass. Both of these compounds contain oxygen. Compounds that are made of only carbon and hydrogen are known as hydrocarbons. These are the building blocks of petroleum-based fuels. Scientists are working to make biofuels copy the properties of gasoline and diesel for a more flexible and efficient renewable fuel.

"Is switchgrass the only grass that will work?" I ask.

"That depends on where you live. Switchgrass grows well in the eastern, southern, and central parts of the United States. Miscanthus is another plant with high cellulose content. It is native to Southeast Asia. It grows well in warm climates."

Tom explains that scientists are experimenting with fast-growing trees such as poplar and willow. But right now they cost more to grow than switchgrass.

A picture forms in my head of my mom stuffing blades of switchgrass into her gas tank. I know carbohydrates

Switchgrass is native to U.S. prairies.

become sugars and sugars become ethanol. I want to know more about how switchgrass turns into the fuel that could power my mom's car. ★

In the morning, Tom takes me to the ethanol factory. We drive past rows and rows of switchgrass before stopping in front of a factory where a truck dumps a load of cut grass into a waiting container.

He introduces me to the factory manager, Laura Martinez, who hands me a hard hat. "You're just in time to make a batch of ethanol," she says.

Laura talks to me as we walk. "Cellulose gives switchgrass its structure, so it is tough stuff," she says. "The first thing we must do is blow apart the cell wall to get to the sugar. The sugar in cellulosic plants is not as easy to get to as in corn plants."

Laura points to a stainless steel tank. "First, we pre-treat the grass with an organic mixture that starts dissolving the tough cell wall. It's similar to the way laundry detergent dissolves stains on your clothes. Then our specially designed enzymes separate the cellulose into individual glucose, or sugar, molecules. A molecule is the smallest unit of a substance that still has the properties of that substance. Microbes eat the glucose molecules and make ethanol. This is called fermentation. After producing

Ethanol refineries convert switchgrass, corn grain, and other biomass into fuel.

the ethanol fuels, we're left with solid plant waste that we use to power the factory."

Laura tells me to think about a car's engine. Gasoline mixes with air in the engine and ignites to release energy. Another way to get at the sugar is to heat biomass to release energy. This method is called gasification.

A NEW FACTORY

British Petroleum (BP) hopes to open a cellulosic farm and ethanol plant in 2014. Located in Highlands, Florida, the farm is expected to grow 20,000 acres (8,000 ha) of grass to produce approximately 36 million gallons (136 million L) of fuel. That is equal to 20,000 football fields of grasses that can reach more than 10 feet (3 m) high! BP will distribute the ethanol to refineries to mix with gasoline.

Unfortunately, Laura says, there are problems with both processes. "The factories require lots of money to build and maintain. In fact, it's too expensive to produce ethanol from switchgrass on a large scale, at least right now."

I guess what Laura is trying to tell me is that no energy source is perfect. I thank Laura and Tom. I'm looking forward to learning more about other types of biofuels. ★

Today I am visiting a research facility in New Hampshire. Here, researchers are studying making biofuels out of **algae**. I know algae range in size from huge seaweeds to tiny organisms floating on the water's surface. The pond scum on the water's surface is the best for biofuels because of its oil content. I imagine my mom pumping pond scum into her car. Algae seem about as far from biofuels as we can get. I am interviewing researcher Emma Hurley to get the whole scoop.

Could algae power your family's car someday?

I meet with Emma at the research center. Algae are growing in wall-sized tanks. But Emma takes me outside to a small wooded area behind the center. A small pond is covered with floating green plants that look like slime. "Algae are not fussy creatures," she tells me. "All they need are water, sunlight, and carbon dioxide to grow."

"Do they use photosynthesis?" I ask.

"Yep," Emma says. "Algae love carbon dioxide. Some algae farms are even built next to factories that produce a lot of carbon dioxide."

I think back to my visits to Mary's cornfield and Tom's switchgrass field.

"Is algae converted to ethanol too?" I ask.

Emma shakes her head. "Nope. We turn algae into **biodiesel**. Some algae contain fat. We can press approximately 75 percent of the fat out. This is like squeezing juice from an orange. The rest can be pulled out with a special chemical. The fatty oil taken from the algae can be used to create biodiesel."

"Is biodiesel better than ethanol?" I ask.

Emma grins, "It could be! Right now, ethanol is the only biofuel produced on a large scale. Algae-based fuel costs more than regular gasoline because algae aren't as easily available as fossil fuels. Plus, we're still trying to

ALGAE FOR THE PIGS

Scientists in New York have replaced soybean meal in livestock feed with the algae left over from biofuel production. Once the fat is harvested from algae for biofuel, scientists are left with no-fat algae that make for very healthy food. Algae may not sound tasty to us. But pigs and chickens love them. This practice also transforms biofuel waste into valuable food for farm animals. It might also help free up valuable farmland for the production of human food.

figure out the best time to grow algae. We need to know how much water they need. We need to find the right time to harvest the algae. We want them to have as much oil as possible. **Bacteria** and other pests can contaminate algae pools. We need to find a way to protect our crop."

Emma goes on, "Right now, an algae-growing biodiesel factory couldn't even come close to making enough fuel to meet our energy needs. But algae research continues. Some airlines are experimenting with a blend of petroleum-based jet fuel and biofuel from algae oil. As long as researchers keep working and scientists keep experimenting, algae-based fuel will keep getting better." ★

Algae can make for healthy food for pigs.

Way to go! You've learned what biofuels are, how they are used now, and how they may be used tomorrow. You know biofuels are made of biomass. Corn grain is easy to grow. But corn also uses prime farmland that could produce food. Grasses such as switchgrass do not compete with our food supply. But the sugar is more difficult and expensive to access. Algae have the potential to create eco-friendly biofuels. But right now we cannot produce nearly enough algae-based biofuels. You've learned that while biofuels research has come a long way, scientists have not yet found the perfect biofuel. The search continues! Congratulations on completing your mission!

CONSIDER THIS

★ Give some examples of biomass around your home.

★ Explain the steps to convert corn to ethanol.

★ Develop a list of ways you can decrease the amount of carbon you and your family add to the environment.

You could make the next big discovery in biofuels!

★ Think about how switchgrass is converted to ethanol. Use the carbon cycle to explain the process.

★ Name some of the problems with developing algae-based biofuel.

algae (AL-jee) single- or multi-celled organisms that live in the water and carry out photosynthesis

bacteria (bak-TEER-ee-uh) single-celled organisms that can only be seen with a microscope

biodiesel (BYE-oh-dee-zuhl) a clean-burning alternative fuel made from biomass

carbohydrate (kahr-buh-HYE-drate) an organic compound that contains carbon, oxygen, and hydrogen molecules

cellulose (SEL-yuh-lohs) a carbohydrate found in the cell walls of green plants that gives a plant its strength and rigid structure

enzyme (EN-zime) a protein that speeds up a chemical reaction in a living organism

greenhouse gas (GREEN-hous gas) a gas that traps heat in the atmosphere

organic (or-GAN-ik) material from living things

photosynthesis (foh-toh-SIN-this-sis) a process through which carbon dioxide, water, and light are converted to energy for plants

protein (PROH-teen) a complex substance necessary to life on Earth

LEARN MORE

BOOKS

Peterson, Christine. *Alternative Energy*. New York:
Children's Press, 2004.

Povey, Karen D. *Biofuels*. San Diego: KidHaven Press, 2006.

Solway, Andrew. *Biofuels*. Pleasantville, NY: Gareth
Stevens, 2008.

WEB SITES

Alliant Energy Kids

http://www.alliantenergykids.com/
EnergyandTheEnvironment/RenewableEnergy/022398

Learn more about the different types of biomass and
what they can be used for.

Energy Kids

http://www.eia.gov/kids/energy.cfm?page=biomass_home-
basics-k.cfm#top-container

Visit this site for biomass facts, pictures, and
activities to share with your friends.

Kids and Energy

http://www.kids.esdb.bg/biomass.html

Check out another resource for kids who want to learn
more about biofuels.

BIOMASS COFFEE CAN

Collect grass clippings, leaves, and fallen flower petals in an old coffee can. Add a few drops of water. Then stir around in the can until the biomass is damp. Cut an X in the middle of the can's cover. Read a thermometer, and record the room temperature. Then insert the thermometer through the cover and into the biomass. Check the temperature of the biomass several times a day for a week. What do you notice about the temperature? Why is this happening?

DISCOVER YOUR CARBON FOOTPRINT

The amount of greenhouse gases you produce is sometimes called your carbon footprint. With an adult's help, visit an online carbon footprint calculator. Examine your results. Where can you reduce emissions? Can you hang laundry in the sun instead of running the clothes dryer? What about growing your own food to reduce driving trips to the grocery store? What are other things you could do to reduce emissions?

INDEX

ABOUT THE AUTHOR

Patricia Newman is the author of several books for children, including *Jingle the Brass*, a Junior Library Guild Selection and a Smithsonian-recommended book; and *Nugget on the Flight Deck*, a California Reading Association Eureka! Silver Honor Book for Nonfiction.

ABOUT THE CONSULTANTS

Leith Nye has a passion for renewable energy, plants and science education. His position in education and outreach at the Great Lakes Bioenergy Research Center fuels all of those interests. In his spare time, he gardens, explores local trails, and identifies wildflowers.

Marla Conn is a reading/literacy specialist and an educational consultant. Her specialized consulting work consists of assigning guided reading levels to trade books, writing and developing user guides and lesson plans, and correlating books to curriculum and national standards.